LETTERS TO MY CORPORATE SISTERS VOLUME 2

Featuring
YVONNE WILBORN

Stories of Endurance, Elevation, and Encouragement

Visionary Dr. Elizabeth A. Carter

A.A.P.P.E.A.L.

AN ABSOLUTE PASSION FOR PERFORMANCE,
ENGAGEMENT, ANALYTICS AND LEADERSHIP

Disclaimer: The methods and stories described within this book are the authors' personal thoughts. They are not intended to be a definitive set of instructions. The advice and strategies contained herein may not be suitable for every situation. You may discover there are other methods and materials to accomplish the same result. The authors have made every effort to ensure the accuracy of the information within this book was correct at the time of publication. The authors do not assume and hereby disclaims any liability to any party for any loss, damage, or disruption caused by errors or omissions, whether such errors or omissions result from accident, negligence, or any other cause.

Publisher : AAPPEAL, LLC, Cranberry Township, PA

https://www.eac-aappeal.com

Cover design by Amir N Graphics

ISBN - 978-1-960727-12-1

Published: August 2024

Dedicated to those who feel unheard, unseen and are struggling being your authentic self. We see you; we hear you; we love you; we are the bullhorns that amplify your voice and champion your journey.

TABLE OF CONTENTS

FOREWORD

BY TIANA VON JOHNSON, DBA

Dear Sisters,

As I sit to write this foreword for the powerful anthology "Letters to My Corporate Sisters," I am reminded of the remarkable journeys women undertake in the corporate world. This collection, presented and hosted by the dynamic Elizabeth "Dr. E" Carter, serves as a framework of endurance, elevation, and encouragement for all women striving for excellence. Dr. E's unwavering commitment to empowering women has inspired countless individuals to reach new heights in their careers and personal lives, which is why I encourage you to read this book. This is more than just a collection of letters; it is a testament to the resilience and strength of women who navigate the complexities of the corporate world. Each letter serves as a source of inspiration, offering insights and advice from those who have walked the path and triumphed over adversity.

Endurance is a theme that resonates deeply throughout this book and for me personally. Having gone through the corporate world and trying to figure out where I belong, I have often questioned whether balancing my corporate career and my entrepreneurial passion would work. The traditional norms of life often dictate staying put, but like me, many of us strive for more. I wanted the safety of my corporate human resources job, but I also wanted the risk of doing whatever I put my mind to. This led me to become the first and only African American female real estate broker-owner on Wall Street, generating over one million dollars in revenue in my first year at only 27 years of age. From there, I became an entrepreneurial powerhouse, motivational speaker, author, and coach to thousands of entrepreneurs around the world. I share this to remind you that you can do anything you set your mind to.

However, do not only take it from me. Take it from the other experts in this book. Their stories are those of resilience and hope. They remind us that perseverance is crucial in the face of challenges, underscoring the importance of staying the course even when the journey seems hard. I applaud those women who, whether they have one year or thirty years in their corporate job, have stayed the course, remained committed, and did the work necessary to thrive in the corporate arena. I also have a special place in my heart for those women who have figured out how to work from 9:00 to 5:00 in their jobs and then from 5:00 to 9:00, tapping into their entrepreneurial passion. It is not easy, but to those who have figured it out, I salute you.

Elevation is another key theme emphasized in this book. The letters highlight the significance of striving for continuous growth and advancement. They remind us that elevation is not just about climbing the corporate ladder but also about uplifting others along the way. We must take others with us on the journey and pull up those sisters who may not know how. In turn, we will be blessed with greater success.

Encouragement, the third pillar of this anthology, is perhaps the most crucial. The support and motivation found in these letters are a testament to the power of sisterhood. They remind us that we are never alone on our journey and that the encouragement of our peers can propel us forward in ways we never imagined. So, I encourage you, even when you do not feel encouraged, to keep pushing forward, even when you feel you cannot.

"Letters to My Corporate Sisters" is a call to action for all women in the corporate world. It urges us to embrace our strength, strive for elevation, and support one another unconditionally. As you read these letters, may you find the endurance to overcome obstacles, the inspiration to elevate yourself and others, and the encouragement to keep moving forward.

With heartfelt gratitude and admiration,

Tiana Von Johnson, DBA

Tiana Von Johnson also known as the MotivateHER, generated her first million dollars at only 27 years old. She is an entrepreneurial powerhouse, motivational speaker, inspirational music artist, and film producer, with her very own docu-film MotivateHER Vol. 1 Therapy streaming on Amazon Prime Video, a real estate broker and mogul in NYC for over a decade, author, luxury handbag designer, motivational board game inventor, holder of six degrees including a Doctor of Business Administration, and a business and personal development coach to thousands of entrepreneurs around the world. Tiana has been featured in countless media outlets, including Black Enterprise, The Real Deal, Crain's New York Business, Curbed, Yahoo Finance, Cheddar News, and more. Additionally, she made her mark in television by producing "Powerhouse," a show that was picked up by NBC Universal early in her career. While Tiana is already a powerful force, she strongly believes she is just getting started!

INTRODUCTION

BY ELIZABETH "DR. E" CARTER, PHD

Compilation Visionary of Letters to My Corporate Sisters

Corporate Executive, Educator, Coach, Speaker, 8x Best Selling Author, PhD in education specializing in training and performance improvement.

Dear Sisters,

A year has passed since the first volume of Letters to My Corporate Sisters, and the world has continued to evolve, presenting new challenges and opportunities for women in corporate spaces. The pandemic has reshaped our working environments, and recent social movements have further highlighted the need for equity and inclusion. These changes have underscored the importance of sharing our stories and experiences.

The loss of both my parents in 2023 has deeply impacted my perspective on life and career. Their passing reminded me of the brevity of life and the importance of making decisions that align with our true selves. It has reinforced my commitment to push beyond fears and to encourage other women to do the same. There are so many hidden stories of resilience and triumph that need to be told, and I am more determined than ever to bring them to light.

Reflecting on my corporate journey, I recognize that the decisions I made were often influenced by a desire to please others and by societal pressures. Yet, despite these influences, I own my choices and am proud of the path I've taken. I now understand that it's essential to prioritize my own well-being and aspirations, making choices that support my health, happiness, and ability to serve others.

As you read these letters, I invite you to reflect on your own journey. What has shaped you to be who you are today? Whether it's your family, friends, co-workers, leaders, clergy, or strangers, every experience contributes to your growth. These letters aim to provide insights and answers, empowering you to face challenges with confidence and to excel in your career.

Sisters, the world is changing, and so are we. Armed with knowledge, resilience, and the courage to pursue our dreams, we will not only see the world change but be the change-makers ourselves.

I extend my deepest gratitude to the incredible women who contributed to this volume. Together, we tackle new and tougher issues, with your voices forming the foundation of this movement. A collective force is essential to empower, educate, and enlighten our peers, leaders, mentors, mentees, minorities, and majorities. We must speak up even when we feel muted, show up even when we feel invisible, and showcase ourselves even when the applause is silent.

Let these letters be lessons for you. Enjoy the book, and please share your thoughts on how it has helped you transform your professional or personal life.

If you have a story you wish to share with our corporate sisters, write a letter! If you wish to participate in the next volume, please send an email to info@DrElizabethCarter.com, place the words – 'Letters to My Corporate Sisters- Next Volume' in the subject line, and we can discuss the opportunity.

Yours in sisterhood,

Dr. E

Elizabeth "Dr. E" Carter, PhD

Your Corporate Elevation Strategist

CEO and Founder: AAPPEAL, LLC (An Absolute Passion for Performance, Engagement, Analytics and Leadership)

Founder of the Elevate Your Value Summit

Founder of the Corporate Sisters Network

Host of the Elevate Your Corporate Value with Dr. E Podcast

" Elevating professionals of color from feeling deflated, unsure or confused about their career to being seen, heard, and valued so that they can thrive in the corporate workplace. "

(434) 322-7431

Website: https://eac-aappeal.com

Facebook: http://www.facebook.com/eacaappeal

Instagram: https://www.instagram.com/eacaappeal/

Corporate Sisters Network:

https://www.facebook.com/groups/corporatesistersnetwork

Other books by Dr. Elizabeth A. Carter and AAPPEAL, LLC

Gaining A.C.C.E.S.S. to Lead Yourself: 16 Activities Critical to Continuous Evolution & Success for Self (2019)- Author Dr. Elizabeth A. Carter

Good Days, Bad Days: The Uplifting Journal (2019)- Author Dr. Elizabeth A. Carter

Gaining A.C.C.E.S.S. to Lead Others: 14 Activities Critical to Continuous Evolution & Success for Self (2020)- Author Dr. Elizabeth A. Carter

A Black First (2020)- Author Peter E. Carter, Published by AAPPEAL, LLC

A Black First: The Blackness Continues (2021)- Author Peter E. Carter, Published by AAPPEAL, LLC

Letters to My Corporate Sisters: Stories of Endurance, Elevation and Encouragement (2023)- Visionary Dr. Elizabeth A. Carter

CHAPTER 1

Presenting With Power: Apply C.A.M.O. to Elevate Your Executive Image

BY NAOMI CARRINGTON-HOCKMAN, DTM

"Be yourself, because it takes too much energy to be someone else."

- Naomi Carrington-Hockman, DTM

Dear Sisters,

We all have innate strengths and weaknesses. However, many of us choose to "play small" or less-than when we are in executive situations. Observe yourself at your next meeting. Your boss or supervisor asks for a status update, and you do one of the following things:

Situation One: Fail to toot your own success.

You talk about what everyone else on the "team" did but yourself.

Situation Two: Become the wallflower.

In a situation where information is being provided to you, when it comes to asking questions, you clam up. Even though you have several useful-to-the-group questions for clarification and / or questions for accuracy, you find yourself clamming up. Sometimes the presenter disseminates incorrect information. What do you do? Often, you wait until the meeting is over then try to speak to the presenter off-line.

Situation Three: Provide an inadequate presentation.

You are responsible for disseminating vital information on your area of expertise that you are a subject-matter expert (SME). Despite this being your wheelhouse where you are comfortable, you present in a manner that the audience is left contemplating your credentials.

Presenting yourself in a diminished capacity is a crime to your own humanity. When you do not toot your own horn, no one else will, and even worse your boss and colleagues will not see you as the architect of any success. When you do not ask the questions that had you asked, you know someone else had the same question as well. Once again you are blending into the crowd, and no one will take notice of your smarts, talents, and analytical prowess.

So, what should you do?

Situation One: Fail to toot your own success.

Solution: A subtle way to humble brag is by inserting the phrase "I led the team to… [insert a success or an achievement]…."

Situation Two: Become the wallflower.

Solution: A subtle way to get the presenter to straighten up his or her talking points is by (1) being brave enough to ask the question in the first place. When you are a subject-matter expert (SME) you should feel confident in your ability to command the material and correct any misinformation. (2) "you mentioned x and y could you elaborate on z…." This line of questioning demonstrates that you were paying attention and that you are not showing off or showing up the presenter.

Situation Three: Provide an inadequate presentation.

Solution: In all these situations, how you show up in the world matters. Let me share a story about presentations. In early 2004, I was responsible for delivering an hour-long presentation to over 200 service members in the Army Military Installation formally called Fort Hood, in Central Texas. I had recently returned from a combat tour in Iraq. This made me the subject-matter expert to the scores of servicemembers that were about to deploy to the Iraqi Theater of Operations. Although I thoroughly knew the material, I failed to communicate effectively while delivering the material. I did not know which louder, my knees knocking or my heart pounding. I did not use the gigantic map of Iraq that was on stage with me. I cowered behind the podium and held the podium for dear life. I felt my knees buckle and I did not move away from the podium to use the theater sized stage. I did not maintain eye contact with anyone in the audience.

What could have made my presentation effective and resonate with the audience is some of the following topics on **Presentation Skills.**

Effective communication is always the catalyst to effect change. Consider camouflaging your speaking flaws. Control your jitters, guide your message, and leverage your audience awareness. For more effective communication, apply C.A.M.O. – Confidence; Appearance; Motion; Observation.

Confidence

First, believe you can deliver your message and that the audience will receive it as intended. Do what you need to establish confidence: power poses or pushups to raise energy levels. Meditate and recite reassuring mantras to calm and center yourself. I must hype myself up before giving a presentation to a large audience. I tend to do push-ups (if I am at home and not on a screen). When I am live, I will do calf-raises, where you move your body weight up, onto the balls of your feet, then down onto your heels. This is hard to do in high-heeled shoes, so if you cannot do calf-raises, you can do anything that quietly shifts your body weight, for example stand on one leg, then the other. Power poses have shifting benefits. For example, "the Superwoman" pose is done by placing your hands on your hips, with your feet apart. Doing a power pose before a presentation transfers nervous energy into a productive organized pattern, resulting in better delivery and creditability while presenting.

Appearance

Look the part so you can feel the part. My friend Carlos is a genius with dressing complementary to his speech. While delivering a speech on sowing seeds, he dressed as a gardener. While giving a speech about food, he dressed in an apron, a chef's hat, and held cooking utensils as props. You may not have to go all in with the costumes, but props give the audience's eyes something congruent to what their ears are hearing. Visual learners may not remember what you said but they may remember the sharp suit, or the million-dollar bill you used as a handout.

Motion

Your body speaks. Eighty percent of communication is nonverbal. Control your message. As you speak, be conscious of what your facial expressions and gestures are saying. Even on Zoom or Microsoft Teams, you can convey movement using the virtual "stage." Be aware of your "speaking area" and exploit it when needed. Lean forward for emphasis and be aware that your hands cannot be seen if you are seated, so ensure to elevate intentional hand gestures. One of my favorite sayings is from Linda Clemons: "I cannot hear what you are saying because your body is speaking so loudly." Linda is riffing from Ralph Waldo Emerson who originally said, "What you are does thunder so loudly that it creates dissonance with whatever you happen to be saying." Ensure your body movements and facial gestures align in tone and intonation with the words coming out of your mouth. For example, "my grandmother died" should not be met with a happy dance or jig, unless you really mean it and will explain the exuberance over a solemn situation.

Observation

Read the audience. Live actors always say they feed off the audience. Take cues from the audience. For example, if they are or are not paying attention, or if audience members are on their phones, looking down, you may have an opportunity to shift their attention back to you and your presentation. You must do something to get them engaged and sitting on the edge of their seat to hear what you are going to say or do next.

Read the room. Ask the audience "focused" questions. Do not ask anything so esoteric. Open ended questions can cause the responding audience to go down obscure rabbit holes. I once was in a presentation, and the presenter asked a question as wide as the Grand Canyon. The audience spent five minutes shouting out answers across every topic under the sun. No one hit the mark. When she finally stopped the chaos and confusion, she let us know the specific answer she was looking for. Had she observed the audience she would have had a gauge of the clueless audience and steered that audience to the answer.

Lessons Learned

How you show up in the world matters. Be yourself. You do not have to be in-authentic in corporate situations. What you have to say has value. Your authentic self is enough. Ensure you always present with power and apply C.A.M.O. to elevate your executive image.

Naomi Carrington-Hockman, **DTM**, is a world-renowned transformation expert, international speaker, best-selling author, and philanthropist. With nearly thirty years of military and civilian leadership experience, she excels in guiding presentation skills and change management within large organizations. Semi-retired, Naomi supports the Pentagon as an IT Program Manager.

A combat veteran, she authored "A Major Transformation: 7 Ways to Lead in Any Environment," aimed at helping leaders maximize their potential. Naomi is featured in the first edition of Voices of Change Magazine by Dr. Cheryl Wood. Naomi is a Co-author in Corporate Sisters by Dr. Elizabeth Carter and Mastering Wealth by Master P.

She holds degrees in Psychology, Military Arts and Science, and Project Management, and is pursuing a Doctorate in Information Technology. Naomi enjoys golfing, Toastmasters, and has traveled to over 58 countries. She is a 2024 Presidential Volunteer Service Awardee.

Email: Info@NaomiSpeaks.com

Follow on Social Media:

https://www.instagram.com/naomicarringtonhockman/

DR. ELIZABETH A. CARTER

CHAPTER 2

Breaking the Silence: Unveiling Hidden Challenges of Microaggressions and Societal Pressures

BY ELIZABETH "DR. E" CARTER, PHD

"Not everything that is faced can be changed, but nothing can be changed until it is faced"

- James Baldwin

Dear Sisters,

Imagine the perfect corporate journey. You go to work every day, doing your best. You have *met* all the requirements—you have spent your money, energy, and time building the career you wanted and achieving your goals. You are moving up the corporate ladder without broken rungs, glass ceilings, or concrete ceilings-- only recognitions and promotions. Life is beautiful.

But then, we awaken from that vision, startled that it could be that easy. Because it is not. We know that is just a pipe dream. Quite often, we are experiencing several hidden challenges in the workplace, such as:

- Microaggressions
- Societal pressures

These are two of the many hidden challenges we face in the corporate workplace. Some of these are hidden for some and not for others. I share personal stories, the mental and physical impacts, and strategies that will allow you to break your silence, empowering you to do and be your best.

Microaggressions

Microaggressions are subtle, often unintentional acts, but depending on who says what and how it is received, they can feel very much intentional and discriminatory. These negative messages are often directed at marginalized populations and can be verbal, nonverbal, or environmental. They carry demeaning meta-communications, where offensive messages are concealed, leaving the targets feeling on edge and under scrutiny. This can create an environment filled with distrust, hostility, and invalidation, leading to lost productivity, ill health, and overall inequity.

Types of Microaggressions:

- **Micro Assaults:** Overt slights or insults, often intentional, like racial epithets or purposeful exclusion.

- **Micro Insults:** Prejudiced stereotypes and assumptions about one's intelligence, morality, or association with a particular group.

- **Microinvalidations**: Comments that devalue or deny the lived experiences of marginalized people.

Why Are They Hidden?

Microaggressions are 'hidden' because they are often subtle, indirect, and sometimes unintentional incidents that can easily pass unchallenged. They tend to take the form of jokes, casual remarks, or innocent questions, making them less obvious than overt racism or discrimination. These behaviors reflect a lack of awareness of the experiences of marginalized groups and stem from implicit biases that everyone carries.

From Mistaken Identity to Micro Insult: A Personal Account

I am big on names and make a conscious effort to remember them. About six years ago, I was on the elevator when a peer stepped on it. I greeted him by name, and he excitedly responded with a salutation, including a first name. The problem was that the name he confidently uttered was not mine, it was another Black woman's name.

I corrected him, which we should (I encourage you to do that as many times as needed). Usually, a person would just apologize and close the interaction. But this conversation continued. "Oh my goodness! I am so sorry, you and (insert other name) look remarkably similar. You ladies have the benefit of 'flexible hairstyles,' I don't have that option," he said, pointing to his balding head. Implying that Black women are interchangeable is a subtle, yet hurtful microaggression. It's a common experience, and many of us often question if we're overreacting. However, it's crucial to recognize these incidents as harmful and to speak up when possible.

Societal Pressures

The battle we have with ourselves is about balancing career aspirations with societal and even family expectations. When we think about careers for women, some roles we were traditionally steered towards include human resources, nursing, teaching, or being a stay-at-home spouse.

Growing up, my family had clear expectations. My dad, from Trinidad, wanted me to be a lawyer and my brother to be a doctor. I was so focused on becoming something that was not me because of these expectations. The same thing happens at work; someone tells you, "Oh, you have great skills; we would love for you to be in HR." No one ever says, "Hey, we would love for you to be in engineering or technology." We must take risks and move past the expectation that women only belong in certain industries. So, I will ask you: Are you in an industry that you were steered towards or one you truly want to be in?

Why Are They Hidden?

Gender stereotypes, biases, and career interests, and expectations, are 'hidden' challenges because they often operate subconsciously and are embedded in workplace culture. These can make them difficult to identify and address. Unconscious biases can lead managers to have different expectations for women compared to their male counterparts. Addressing these challenges requires conscious effort to recognize and change these underlying attitudes and practices.

When Ambition Meets Bias: My Struggle for Success

After seven years of job hopping, after abandoning my false aspirations of becoming a lawyer, I found my strength and skills aligned in the finance department of an insurance company. Despite being a minority in several categories, I was determined to excel and move into the managerial ranks. After years of hard work and overcoming societal expectations, I landed a managerial position. However, a microaggression from a senior leader made me question my abilities and place in the industry. The Finance leader called me to his office because of an item I missed in the process I was overseeing. He was originally from the South and emulated the profile of a typical finance leader, as the slogan says; pale, stale and male. As I explained the situation, he rudely waved his hand to stop me, leaned towards me, and said, "Well, lit'le lady, maybe finance ain't the place for you." His dismissive comment undermined my confidence and highlighted the challenges women face in male-dominated fields. The experience took a toll on my mental health, ultimately leading to my departure from the company.

The Mental and Physical Impacts of Hidden Challenges

Chronic exposure to microaggressions and the pressure to conform to societal expectations can lead to a range of mental health challenges. These include increased stress, anxiety, depression, and lower self-esteem. The constant devaluation and unfair treatment often experienced by women can also contribute to feelings of imposter syndrome.

The mental toll of these challenges can manifest in physical symptoms as well. Sleep disturbances, headaches, and exhaustion are common. Prolonged stress can also lead to more serious health issues such as cardiovascular problems, weakened immune function, and chronic conditions.

It's crucial to recognize that these impacts are not isolated incidents but rather systemic issues affecting countless women. By acknowledging the severity of these challenges, we can begin to address them effectively and create a more supportive and equitable workplace for all.

Personally, I have experienced firsthand the debilitating effects of these hidden challenges. The mental and physical toll has been immense. However, it is through sharing our stories and supporting one another that we can begin to heal and create lasting change.

My Sisters,

Please do not go any longer suffering these hidden challenges. I offer eight solutions that will free you to move forward with power and strength.

Strategies to Overcome Microaggressions

- **Respond:** Consider the importance of the issue and the relationship. You can let it go, call it out immediately, or bring it up later. Even though it is against the law for a person to retaliate, the relationship could majorly impact the team and the work.

- **Seek Support:** Talk to peers or someone in a position of authority if needed. It is important to have a support system.

- **Encourage Allies:** As leaders, encourage allies to intervene when they witness microaggressions, which can help create a supportive environment.

- **Raise Awareness:** Engage in open conversations to foster understanding within your organization.

- **Educate:** Be firm but polite in correcting the perpetrator in the areas where their generalized assumption does not speak to the entire population they reference.

Strategies to Balance Career Aspirations with Societal/Family Expectations

- **Embrace Your True Self:** Challenge societal norms, honor your values and passions, and practice self-compassion to balance personal authenticity and societal expectations.

- **Reflect on Norms**: Reflect on whether societal norms serve your authentic self and make conscious choices that align with your truth. Did you know that 66% of the workforce is either disengaged or not engaged? If you are stressed or unhappy, address the issue and consider moving to a place where you are valued.

- **Be Courageous:** Have the courage to make a change, be authentic and accept that not everyone will understand or resonate with your choices. And be unapologetic!!

Conclusion: Empowering Our Journey

My Sisters,

We have journeyed through the often-unseen terrain of microaggressions and societal pressures that shape our professional and personal lives. These hidden challenges can be insidious, slowly eroding our confidence and well-being. Yet, by breaking the silence and bringing these issues to light, we empower ourselves and each other to create change.

In addition to the strategies, I leave you with these affirmations to carry forward:

1. I have the confidence and tools to call out what I see and hear.

2. I have allies (or I am an ally) that intervene(s) when witnessing microaggressions.

3. I embrace my true self and honor my values and passions.

4. "Why" is a great question, and "Why Not" is my superpower.

Let us move forward together, breaking barriers, shattering ceilings, and rewriting the narrative of what it means to be successful women in corporate spaces. Our journey is not just for us but for every sister who follows.

References

For more insight into microaggressions, please refer to these resources:

- Healthline on Microaggressions.
  https://www.healthline.com/health/microaggressions

- Psychology Today on Microaggressions.
  https://www.psychologytoday.com/intl/basics/microaggression

- APA Podcasts on Microaggressions.
  https://www.apa.org/news/podcasts/speaking-of-psychology/microaggressions

- Medical News Today on Microaggressions and Health.

https://www.medicalnewstoday.com/articles/microaggressions-how-and-why-do-they-impact-health

- Harvard Gazette on Microaggressions and Mental Illness. https://news.harvard.edu/gazette/story/2019/11/microaggressions-and-their-role-in-mental-illness/

- Harvard Business Review on Women in the Workplace. https://hbr.org/2022/03/research-roundup-how-women-experience-the-workplace-today

Elizabeth "Dr. E" Carter, PhD founded AAPPEAL in 2016 with a mission to elevate corporate professionals from uncertainty to increased recognition, confidence, and fulfillment in their careers. With an "<u>A</u>bsolute <u>P</u>assion for <u>P</u>erformance, <u>E</u>ngagement, <u>A</u>nalytics, and <u>L</u>eadership," Dr. E helps clarify how these four pillars are crucial for career success.

Committed to addressing the underrepresentation of women and minorities in managerial roles, she draws from over 25 years in Corporate Finance, working for Allstate, The Hartford, AIG, Farmers, and Blue Cross/Blue Shield. Despite being often the only woman of color in the room, she remains energized and dedicated to driving change.

Dr. E is also a speaker, trainer, coach, 8x Best-Selling Author, Founder of the Elevate Your Value Summit and Corporate Sisters Network, and host of the Elevate Your Corporate Value with Dr. E Podcast.

Women seeking career advancement and empowerment are encouraged to contact Dr. E for support and guidance.

Website: https://www.eac-aappeal.com

Facebook, Instagram: eacaappeal

Email: info@DrElizabethCarter.com

DR. ELIZABETH A. CARTER

CHAPTER 3

Now That You Have The Seat At The Table, What's Next?

BY TYNINA LUCAS

"Oh, that You would bless me indeed, and enlarge my territory, that Your Hand would be with me, and that You would keep me from evil, that I may not cause pain!"

- I Chronicles 4:10

Dear Sisters,

I hope you are well as you read this chapter and will find my words uplifting and empowering, giving you confidence during your career journey.

More than twenty years ago, I embarked on my professional journey in my first job out of college, joining a small telecom company with aspirations of building a successful career. However, fate had other plans as the company succumbed to bankruptcy, throwing me into uncertainty at the onset of my career.

The following year was quite significant as I received Christ as my savior. This transformative event not only enlightened me from a spiritual perspective but also instilled in me a newfound resilience to face challenges. Despite the tumultuous external and economic environment amidst the chaos of the post-9/11 world, I persevered, determined to carve out a place for myself in the corporate world. As a result, I was given the opportunity to join a large global company, which presented its own set of challenges. As the youngest and only minority woman on the team, I was often overlooked. However, I refused to be defined by stereotypes or limitations imposed by others. Given tasks based on my gender and age, I saw each challenge as an opportunity to showcase my abilities.

Through diligent work and unwavering determination, I earned opportunities to present to high-ranking executives, leading to promotions and greater responsibilities within various roles in different companies.

As a minority woman in a predominantly male-dominated world, I recognized the importance of advocating for diversity and inclusion. From attending prestigious events to engaging in board meetings with top executives, I seized every opportunity to demonstrate my value and abilities and champion diversity within the organizations where I worked.

In moments where authenticity mattered most, I remained true to myself. Whether attending board meetings or engaging in conversations with executive leaders, I approached each interaction with authenticity and professionalism, earning respect and recognition along the way.

Acknowledging the prevalence of imposter syndrome, I learned to silence the doubts and insecurities that plagued my mind. Instead, I focused on demonstrating my abilities and the value I brought to the table, confident in my capacity to excel and thrive in any situation. When asked to participate in high-level meetings or accept tasks for various reasons, instead of harping on why I was selected, I directed my mindset to how to add value. We must acknowledge that in some cases, you may have been chosen to participate because of your gender or race to demonstrate a propensity for diversity and inclusion; however, regardless of the reason you are asked to participate, you were given a seat at the table, and now that you have that seat, you need to prove that you are worthy of being there and staying there.

Very early in my career, I was asked to present to the Global SVP and CIO within the organization in which I worked; I was chosen to conduct this presentation to demonstrate the work that I had done on a specific initiative; however, I knew deep down that was selected for this task because I was double minority to exhibit the organization's commitment to uplifting diverse employees in front of executive leadership. At the time, I was the only African American female in my department. Although it was apparent why I was asked to present, I did not let that discourage or make me fearful. Instead, when informed of the request, I researched and reviewed my material, practiced my presentation skills, and went shopping. Since I was given this opportunity, I would take it and show them I knew what I was talking about and would dress like I was supposed to be there.

On the day of the presentation, I was prepared for whatever questions the executives had for me. However, after I began my presentation, my manager interrupted me and thought it was necessary to speak on my behalf. Immediately after he interrupted, the Global SVP interjected, said, "Let her speak, " and gently told me to continue my presentation. I then continued my presentation and received recognition from executives regarding my work. I subsequently received recommendations and approvals from that same executive team to be promoted to the next level shortly after that. I was later promoted twice within the next two to three years. Despite my manager's urging to speak for me, the Global SVP wanted to hear what I had to say. I had brought my authentic self to the meeting. I convinced those leaders that I deserved to be there not because I was a minority but because of my capabilities, which led to executive sponsorship and promotion.

Lessons I learned that I share with you

1) *While I am at the table, I will be my authentic self.* Being your authentic self in a professional setting does not mean presenting the same "self" that you would with your close friends and family; it does mean being honest, doing your research, and adding value while you are at the table. It also means not letting fear hold you back and acknowledging that God has not given you the spirit of fear. Still, He has given you power, love, and a sound mind (2 Timothy 1:7). The Merriam-Webster dictionary defines power as the ability to act or produce an effort. Therefore, you must use your God-given "power" to show your worth. You can do that by doing your research and obtaining an in-depth understanding of the topics to be discussed to effectively ask questions and insert insightful observations and remarks, allowing you to engage in rational discussion with those at the table.

2) *I will be respectful and approach each conversation with love and understanding.* Regardless of why you were included in the meeting, acknowledge those present and respect them despite what you think they may have initially thought about you. Finally, engage in the conversation with a sound mind. According to the Merriam-Webster dictionary, "sound" means solid, firm, secure, reliable, or stable. Remember, it is essential that you not let people, new responsibilities, or situations overwhelm you. Your research, your faith, and confidence in

your abilities will help you remain on solid ground. Irrespective of why you were brought to the table, you must remain confident that the value you add will enable you to stay at the table and elevate you to the next level.

Reflecting on my journey thus far, I am grateful for the challenges that have shaped me into who I am today. Through resilience, determination, and unwavering faith in God, I am navigating the complexities of the corporate world, emerging stronger and more empowered than ever before. Furthermore, I appreciate those who have given me opportunities to showcase my ability and supported me along the way.

I will leave you with the following excerpt from "Suits," spoken by the character, Jessica Pearson, to her former manager when she discovered that her status as a double minority may have influenced hiring at the firm. Within the quote below, Jessica emphasized her recognition of what the "asterisk" meant next to her name. She confronted the unpleasant reality of being selected for her position based on her identity rather than her qualifications or merits alone. "When I saw that asterisk next to my name, it made me sick to my stomach because, in one second, I understood how you would always see me. So that card was a thank you because if I hadn't felt sick, then I might not have worked as hard as I did to get where I am today. You woke the dragon, Charles; how do you like me now". - Jessica Pearson, Managing Partner from Suits. Although Jessica is a fictional character, this resonated with me as her response encapsulated the determination and resilience required to overcome systemic impediments and thrive in environments where differences are sometimes perceived as limitations. Although the seat may have been given because of your identity, you must use your abilities, power, love, and sound mind to embolden you to stay and flourish despite the circumstances.

References

- Merriam-Webster, Inc. (2024). Merriam-Webster Dictionary Online. Retrieved https://www.merriam-webster.com/about-us/faq#:~:text=The%20first%20Merriam%2DWebster%20dictionary,Polk%20and%20General%20Zachary%20Taylor.

- OpenAI. (2024). ChatGPT. Retrieved from https://chat.openai.com.

- Unknown (2024). King James Version. 2 Timothy 1:7. Bible.

Tynina Lucas is currently Vice President, Procurement & Strategic Sourcing at EmblemHealth and has over 17 years of Procurement Leadership experience working for large global organizations and large health plans. During her career, Tynina has conceptualized and created Procurement departments within organizations where no prior Procurement organization existed. Under her leadership, Tynina's teams have consistently exceeded cost reduction goals and spear-headed changes including the deployment of Supplier Diversity Programs.

Tynina's expertise includes negotiations, strategic sourcing, global sourcing, and strategic planning etc. Her sourcing experience encompasses nearly every category, including IT, Health Services, Facilities, Corporate Services, Chemicals, Pharmacy, Water Treatment, Waste Services etc.

She has a bachelor's degree in information science from the University of Pittsburgh, and an MBA from Trident University International.

She may be reached at tyninalucas@gmail.com

CHAPTER 4

Inspired by Challenges:

The Story of an Immigrant Black Woman

BY DR. STELLA ONUOHA-OBILOR,

DRPH, MD, MPH, RN, CPHQ, CCM

"I can do all things through Christ who strengthens me."

- Philippians 4:13

Dear Sisters,

Friends always tell me that my story is inspiring, and that my resilience and faith are admirable. So, I am delighted to share the same story with you. My experiences have undoubtedly shaped my leadership style and empathy, making me a strong and compassionate leader.

When I arrived at John F. Kennedy Airport, I realized I had left my family in Nigeria to start a new chapter in the United States. It was a bittersweet moment - I was happy to reunite with my husband but sad to leave my mother and siblings behind. I struggled with homesickness and loneliness for weeks, despite being with my husband and his family. I questioned my decision and worried about my future. However, my faith in God's presence and guidance gave me strength.

Adapting to the new culture was a shock, and I had to relearn many things. I faced challenges with language, dietary changes, and cultural differences. Some people were kind, while others were unkind and made assumptions about my background. Despite these challenges, I motivated myself to succeed, knowing I was better than my excuses.

As a full-time working mother of four, I pursued my master's in public health and Doctor of Public Health degrees online from Walden University. I completed both programs in 2015 and 2017, respectively. Through these experiences, I realized that immigrant black women from West African countries face unique challenges in the United States, including corporate world barriers, health issues, and dietary acculturation. These challenges have shaped my leadership style, making me more empathetic, compassionate, and kind. I value diversity and putting people first.

To my corporate sisters, especially Black immigrant women, I offer this advice: never relinquish your dreams. Initially, your decision to pursue a new path may seem misguided, and not everyone will be willing to support you. Even close friends and relatives may view you as a disappointment, but don't let that discourage you. Set clear goals and work tirelessly to achieve them. Embrace risk-taking, recognizing that failures provide valuable learning opportunities. View challenges as catalysts for growth and development. Each "no" you encounter should propel you to the next level.

In the corporate world, confidently share your accomplishments with peers and senior leaders. Be your own advocate and cheerleader, ensuring your contributions are recognized. Seek feedback, including 360 feedback, to address blind spots and improve. Embrace feedback as a gift, even when unexpected. However, don't allow ineffective leaders to use feedback to diminish your worth.

Lead with empathy, compassion, and mutual respect, prioritizing your team's well-being. When you value and respect your team, they will go above and beyond for you. Remember, people may forget your words and actions, but they will always recall how you made them feel. Lead with kindness, leaving a lasting impact.

I want to encourage you to rise above your challenges and not let them define your potential. I've faced numerous obstacles, but I chose to focus on my goals instead of letting struggles hold me back. My experiences have shaped me and made me more resilient.

In the corporate world, my challenges made me a better leader. I strive to treat others with kindness and respect, unlike some leaders I've encountered. I'm my own biggest cheerleader, and I'm not afraid to stand up for myself and share my achievements with humility and professionalism.

Remember, no matter how hard you work, you need good sponsors to advocate for you behind closed doors. Excel in your work and make it easy for others to support you.

As a leader, I believe in authenticity and treating my team with kindness. I strive to create a positive work environment where everyone feels valued. Don't try to fit in; be yourself. Embrace your identity and don't let others define you.

To my fellow immigrant Black women in the corporate world, I see you. Be your amazing selves and don't try to conform. You will thrive in an environment where you are celebrated, not tolerated. Keep shining!

As leaders, it's crucial to remain connected with our teams even as we grow and evolve. While our knowledge and perspectives may change, we must stay relatable and relevant to effectively share our insights and help others grow. This approach ensures our new ideas are well received, leading to real growth and change.

As the saying goes, "We teach what we know, but we reproduce who we are." Leaders must prioritize self-discovery and continuous learning to inspire growth in others. Investing in ourselves allows us to develop others, fostering a culture of mutual respect and continuous improvement.

The Law of Awareness from John Maxwell's 15 Invaluable Laws of Growth emphasizes the importance of self-awareness in personal growth. By asking ourselves quality questions, we gain a deeper understanding of ourselves, our strengths, and our goals. This self-awareness is the foundation of empathic and compassionate leadership.

As someone who has overcome numerous challenges, I'm passionate about empowering others to cultivate self-awareness and follow their hearts. By sharing my journey and lessons learned, I aim to help others break free from limitations, trust their intuition, and live authentic lives. Remember, personal growth precedes team growth. Let's commit to our own improvement and set a powerful example for our teams to excel.

According to Adam Grant, renowned author, professor, and organizational psychologist, fostering respect and support for your team is crucial. Leaders who neglect to do so will inevitably face a decline in both morale and performance. Consistently abrasive behavior will stifle innovation, as team members will only do the bare minimum, rather than sharing their best ideas. This toxic culture will ultimately harm your company's bottom line. Instead, lead with kindness and integrity, and watch your team thrive. Your future success depends on it. By prioritizing a supportive and respectful work environment, you'll encourage creativity, collaboration, and excellence, driving your organization towards achievement and prosperity.

You are the star of your own life show! Every decision and action propel your story forward. Remember, you have the power to control your narrative, not external events. As Marcus Aurelius said, "You have power over your mind—not outside events. Realize this, and you will find strength."

Don't let others' expectations dictate your script. Take control of your storyline by setting your own goals and pursuing them with determination. As CS Lewis said, "You can't go back and change the beginning, but you can start where you are and change the ending."

Celebrate your individuality, unique talents, and don't shy away from the spotlight. Your journey is unlike anyone else's, and that's your greatest asset. Mark Twain said, "The secret of getting ahead is getting started." So take that first step, write your own dialogue, and make each scene memorable.

Embrace your role as the protagonist with confidence. Every star has the potential to illuminate the world in their own way. Keep shining!

Through my challenges, I've come to realize that failure is not only a natural part of growth but also a valuable learning tool. As Stephen McCranie aptly puts it, "For every skill, the master has failed more times than the beginner has even tried." Failure is not the opposite of success; it's a steppingstone to achieving it.

Here are three compelling reasons why failure is the best teacher:

1. **Failure reveals blind spots**, exposing areas for improvement, and highlighting skills that need refinement. It challenges our

assumptions, uncovers knowledge gaps, and provides a reality check.

2. **Failure builds grit**, strengthening our resolve to succeed. It teaches us to persevere through adversity, work smarter, and develop patience and resilience.

3. **Failure sparks innovation**, encouraging creative problem-solving, challenging the status quo, and driving unique ideas and effective decision-making.

Remember, failure is not the end but the beginning of success. Embrace it as a valuable learning experience. The only true failure is when we stop trying. By reframing our mindset, we can turn failure into a catalyst for success. Let failure be your best teacher and guide you towards achieving your goals.

Finally, my beloved sisters, do not forget that health is wealth, and we need abundance of it. As we navigate our demanding careers, let's remember that health is wealth. It's essential to prioritize self-love and well-being to maintain our physical and mental health, ensuring long-term success and fulfillment.

To achieve this balance, let's establish clear boundaries, practice mindful time management, and incorporate self-care activities into our daily routines. Nurturing our body and mind is crucial, and we can do this through simple practices like exercise, meditation, and healthy eating.

Building a supportive community of peers and mentors is also vital, providing encouragement and guidance during challenging times.

Finally, let's embrace moments of reflection and renewal, taking time to recharge and reconnect with our inner selves.

By prioritizing self-love and well-being, we're not only taking care of ourselves but also becoming more productive, focused, and successful in our careers. Remember, self-love is not selfish - it's essential. Let's empower each other to prioritize our well-being and live a balanced, fulfilling life.

Dr. Stella Onuoha-Obilor is an astute public health physician executive with over 18 years of experience in population health, continuous performance improvement, and change management.

She is a transformational, hands-on Clinical Quality & Population Health Leader with a demonstrated track record of championing a culture of excellence across a health plan and provider footprint, optimizing care delivery and financial performance while prioritizing patient safety and delivering exceptional value. She is known for a strong background in HEDIS, Risk Adjustment, and CMS Stars analytics as well as Population Health Management for over one million Medicare and Medicaid lives. Ensures integration across the enterprise and upholds the quality, safety, and value vision for all associates and patients. Dr. Obilor works collaboratively across matrixed teams with Clinical and Quality Leadership to drive and execute the quality strategy across an enterprise. She has also been recognized by Becker's Healthcare as one of the 231+ Black Healthcare Leaders to know in 2024.

Email: Shawntelobilor@yahoo.com

Instagram: (@doubledoctor_stella)

Twitter (X) : @ObilorDr

LinkedIn: stella-onuoha-obilor-drph-md-mph-rn-cphq-ccm-bb078218

DR. ELIZABETH A. CARTER

CHAPTER 5

Embrace and Rise: The Art of Body Positivity and Self-Love

BY WILLIE MAE STARR-WHITE

"I praise you because I am fearfully and wonderfully made; your works are wonderful; I know that full well."

- Psalm 139:14 (NIV)

Dear Sisters,

This verse is a beautiful reminder of our uniqueness and the divine craftsmanship that shapes each of us!

In the heart of the corporate wilderness, I'm an Office/Facilities manager at a law firm, and like you Corporate Sisters, I am the embodiment of strength, intelligence, confidence, reliability, and compliance. "I AM SUPER WOMAN!" I love my career, yet, in the face of my brilliance, I have been met with the shadows of workplace body shaming and micro-aggressive comments, a challenge to my very presence due to my size. I have felt the exclusion, the whispers, the giggles, and the biting comments that would test the fortitude of any soul.

One day in a moment of vulnerability within the ladies' restroom, I faced the piercing words of a colleague. Her laughter, a jarring sound against the quietness, as she made remarks on my weight that cut deep, "Why do you try? Why do you act like you're not big?"

As I hastily gathered my makeup and made my way out of the restroom, the silence surrounding me seemed suffocating. Every step I took, her laughter echoed in my ears, a constant reminder of the pain she had inflicted upon me. But deep within, a flicker of resilience ignited, urging me to rise above her shallow words.

Seeking solace in the sanctuary of faith that resides in the depths of my being, I found strength in the divine affirmation imprinted on my soul. The words from Psalm 139:14 reverberated through my mind, reminding me of my inherent worth and beauty. I am fearfully and wonderfully made, crafted perfectly in the image of a masterful creator.

With newfound determination, I mustered the courage to reclaim my power. I returned to the restroom, a blazing fire burning within me, ready to confront my callous colleague. In that moment, I stood tall, my poise conveying an unshakable knowledge of my value.

Addressing my colleague, I spoke with unwavering conviction. I declared the truth of our individual masterpiece designs, reminding her that every person deserves respect and dignity. I demanded that she acknowledge the inherent worth we all possess and treat others with the same kindness she would expect for herself.

But as I reflect on that moment, I can't help but wonder: what if I had succumbed to my insecurities? What if I had let her hurtful words define me and erode my self-esteem? The possibilities of shrouded self-doubt loom before me, reminding me of the strength it took to stand up for myself.

Nevertheless, I am grateful for the sanctuary of faith within me that guided me to reclaim my worth. It is a constant reminder that I am more than the words hurled at me, that my true value lies in the unique beauty and resilience that resides deep within my soul. No matter the circumstances, I am fearfully and wonderfully made, deserving of respect, love, and acceptance.

This situation transcends as a mere tale of triumph; it is a jubilation of the unyielding spirit within all of us, nurtured by faith and self-acknowledgment. It serves as a reminder to every individual of their invaluable worth and the exquisite craftsmanship that constitutes their existence. My journey stands as a lighthouse, illuminating the path for those who have felt diminished, whispering courageously, "You are more than enough."

As women, we are hard on ourselves, and sometimes we are shaded with so much negativity, that we forget how beautiful we are. Let this story reverberate as a clarion call of inspiration, affirming that our value is not a reflection of external judgments but a testament to our inherent worth and the sustaining power of our beliefs. Our resilience and confidence in the face of adversity stands as a testament to the inner strength and bravery that we all possess.

The echoes of laughter and mockery still linger in my memory, a cruel reminder of the times when my weight and race became the target of ridicule. I endured the teasing, the harsh words, and the scornful looks, all the while believing that perhaps they were right. I remained silent, a silent witness to my own diminishing self-worth.

"Why should I even try?" This question haunted me as I retreated to the solitude of my home, each evening heavier than the last. Depression was my unwelcome companion, whispering doubts and sowing despair. Yet, within the depths of my vulnerability, a spark of resilience flickered. Each morning, I mustered the courage to face the world anew, to stand tall amidst the storm of judgment.

It was not until I found my voice, a firm and resolute "STOP," that the tide began to turn. I learned to stand up for myself, to reclaim my dignity from the hands of those who sought to belittle me. It was a journey of self-discovery, of realizing that their words did not define me, nor did they hold any truth.

You are not alone, and your worth is immeasurable. Let us stand together, united in our diversity, and say with unwavering conviction, "We are enough, just as we are."

Body Shaming

Body shaming is a scourge that wounds the heart and soul, casting shadows over the beautiful diversity of human forms. Whether it targets our skin, hair, weight, height, race, or any other facet of our physical being, it is an injustice that corrodes our collective self-esteem and inflicts deep psychological pain.

In our daily lives, we encounter a barrage of backhanded compliments, unsolicited advice, and microaggressions. These are not mere words; they are the subtle weapons of a society that has yet to learn to cherish all bodies. They are the threads that weave a tapestry of discrimination, marginalizing those who do not conform to arbitrary standards of beauty. It is our duty to recognize these insidious behaviors and halt them in their tracks, for they have no place in a world that values kindness and respect.

Exclusion based on appearance is a particularly cruel form of rejection, one that sends a message that only certain bodies are worthy of notice and appreciation. It is a message that breeds loneliness and perpetuates inequality, and it must be challenged with every fiber of our being.

To recognize and understand these harmful practices is to take the first step towards building a society that radiates inclusivity, understanding, and emotional support. It is a call to action to create a world where every person is honored and celebrated for their unique self, unbound by the oppressive chains of narrow beauty standards. By embracing the principles of body positivity and actively opposing these damaging behaviors, we stand shoulder to shoulder, supporting one another in the quest for a community that is not just accepting, but loving and nurturing for all. Together, we can transform our world into a haven of compassion and encouragement, where every individual can flourish in the fullness of their being.

Empowerment and Transformation

TODAY, I rise to share a message of empowerment and transformation. "Embrace and Rise: The Art of Body Positivity and Self-Love" is not a mere slogan; it is a revolution, a bold declaration of self-worth that rises above the currents of body shaming.

Corporate Sisters, we are summoned to acknowledge and rejoice in the unique masterpiece that is our form. It is a call to foster self-acceptance and to nurture resilience against societal pressures. We proclaim that our uniqueness is our power, and our diversity, our splendor.

United in this revolution of love and unapologetic authenticity, we are equipped with tools to challenge and change the unrealistic standards set before us. We celebrate diversity, enriching the world with a spectrum of beauty. We cultivate positive environments, laying the foundation for a society that elevates rather than diminishes. Through self-care, we construct a bastion of self-assurance, steadfast and enduring.

Resilience, the cornerstone of this newfound confidence, enables us to surmount obstacles, to grow from setbacks, to adapt, and to persist. It infuses us with a hopeful perspective, empowering us to emerge fortified, self-reliant, and prepared to meet the world with dignity.

Let us carry this message into the future. Let us "Embrace and Rise" in unison, carving a trail of body positivity and self-love that will resonate for ages.

And let us extend this message of body positivity into the halls of our workplaces, through a comprehensive approach that encompasses educating, exemplifying, and fostering an environment of inclusion.

Embrace Your Radiance and Beauty: Fostering Body Positivity in the Workplace

Corporate Sisters, in the dynamic environment of our workplaces, we find an opportunity to cultivate a culture of body positivity that uplifts everyone. We are who we are, no one can change that. God made us uniquely different. Here are some suggestions:

- **Be the Beacon: Embodying Positive Leadership** Envision a leader who doesn't merely lead with words but personifies them. This leader speaks kindly about their own body, celebrating its distinctiveness. Such leaders, our beacons, participate in activities that nurture body confidence. They dance, laugh, and wear their favorite outfits without hesitation. Their authenticity shines, inspiring others to accept their own bodies.

- **Weave the Threads: Incorporating Body-Positive Programs**
  Let's integrate evidence-based programs into our workplace culture. These programs, akin to intricate embroidery, emphasize media literacy. They challenge the inflexible ideals imposed by society. They remind us, "You are more than a reflection; you are resilience." They guide us to discard the yardstick of comparison and gauge our worth in self-love.

- **The Inclusive Quilt: Creating an Accepting Environment**
  Beyond the boardrooms and cubicles, let's broaden our efforts. Picture a quilt sewn together with threads of diversity. Each square symbolizes a different body shape, a unique narrative. We celebrate them all—the curves, the angles, the softness, and strength. We reassess our HR policies, ensuring they protect us from appearance-related bullying. We rectify any microaggressions, creating a safe space for every thread in our quilt.

- **Colors of Wellness: Promoting Health Positively** Our palette transitions from monochrome to vibrant colors. We promote health-enhancing behaviors, not with fear, but with joy. Discussions on mental health flourish like wildflowers, nourishing our minds. We cherish our relationship with food, savoring gratitude with every bite. And movement? It's not a chore; it's a dance—a celebration of our bodies' capabilities.

- **The Symphony of Co-Creation: Encouraging Employee-Led Initiatives** Let's pass the baton to our colleagues. They lead discussions, crafting harmonies of body confidence. Together, we create a symphony of acceptance, resilience, and self-love. We foster spaces where ownership thrives. Our workplace transforms into a sanctuary, where self-confidence blossoms like spring flowers.

Promoting Body Positivity: What Can You Do Personally?

- Promote body diversity in educational materials and media, challenging limited beauty standards.

- Use inclusive language and avoid stereotypes about body size and shape.

- Focus on overall health rather than weight alone, promoting mental well-being and positive relationships with food and exercise.

- Celebrate differences in body types and abilities, fostering acceptance and self-love.

- If you recognize you have been body shaming someone, cease and apologize.

By taking these steps, we can contribute to a more inclusive and accepting society where people can feel comfortable and confident in their own bodies, regardless of societal expectations and beauty standards. It is important to remember that everyone deserves respect and dignity, regardless of their physical appearance.

In Summary, Corporate Sisters, as you turn the page, Embrace and Rise…You are a **MASTERPIECE**—an intricately woven tapestry of courage, vulnerability, and grace. Your worth transcends the confines of boardrooms and cubicles. You are fearfully and wonderfully made. Embrace your imperfections and remember: **"I AM BEYOND ENOUGH."**

Willie Mae Starr-White is Your Empathy Messenger, *"Turning Uncertainty into Silver Linings of Hope."* She is a motivational speaker with a passion for inspiring positive change.

For the past 17 years, she has been an active member of Toastmasters International, a community that has nurtured her love for communication and leadership. Through countless speech contests, she has honed her craft, learning that words can transform lives.

Starr-White's journey extends beyond the stage. As the co-author of four best-selling books, she has explored the depths of human resilience, personal growth, and the art of overcoming obstacles. These books are not just ink on paper; they represent shared wisdom, collective experiences, and the unwavering belief that we can all rise above our challenges.

Willie Mae balances her speaking and writing with a presence in the corporate world, spending the past 13 years as the Facilities/Office Services Manager at a prestigious law firm. In this role, she has witnessed the ebb and flow of professional life—the late nights, the early mornings, and the quiet moments when decisions shape destinies.

Are you looking for your silver lining?

Reach out to Willie Mae Starr-White at:

yourempathymessenger@gmail.com

linkedin.com/in/willie-mae-starr-whitea8b51a43

DR. ELIZABETH A. CARTER

CHAPTER 6

Shattering Stereotypes:
Overcoming "Angry Black Woman" and "Ice Queen" Labels

BY WILLIE MAE STARR-WHITE

"Live in harmony, avoiding pride and conceit."

- Romans 12:16

Dear Sisters,

I want to share my journey through the prestigious halls of a top law firm where I was the sole Black woman. I faced two daunting labels: the "Angry Black Woman" and the "Ice Queen." My colleagues whispered that I was too assertive and intimidating, but I drew strength from my family's legacy of resilience and civil rights activism. Determined to rewrite the narrative, I faced these challenges with grace and authenticity, transforming my reputation. My story is one of breaking barriers and embracing our true selves, inspiring us all to challenge stereotypes and redefine professionalism with authenticity and resilience.

Label #1: "The Angry Black Woman"

I sat at my desk, the hum of the fluorescent lights echoing the buzz in my mind. As the only black woman in the prestigious law firm, I felt the weight of expectations—both professional and cultural. My colleagues often whispered about me, their words veiled in concern: "Willie Mae needs more tact," "She's too assertive," "She's unapproachable."

My performance reviews echoed the same refrain. "Willie Mae, you're brilliant, but soften your edges," my supervisor would say. "Clients find you intimidating." I knew what they meant—the stereotype of the "Angry Black Woman" clung to me like a shadow. This was a combat daily.

But I refused to shrink. I grew up watching my grandmother fight for civil rights, my mother break barriers in academia. I carried their legacy—their resilience—in my blood and veins. So, I decided to rewrite the narrative.

One day, during a contract renewal meeting, I faced a formidable opponent—a seasoned attorney known for his condescension. As he belittled my suggestions during the meeting, I took a deep breath. Instead of reacting defensively like everyone expected, I leaned in. "Mr. Thomas," I said calmly, "let's focus on the facts."

My confidence disarmed him. I presented my suggestion with precision, dismantling his suggestions one by one in the meeting. The room fell silent. When I finished, even Mr. Thomas had to concede.

Word spread. my colleagues watched in awe as I navigated the workplace labyrinth with grace and determination. I didn't compromise my authenticity; I amplified it. When co-workers hesitated to work with me, I met their doubts head-on. "I'm here to work," I'd say. "And I'll do it with integrity."

My reputation shifted. People stopped whispering about my "tact" and started seeking my advice. I became a mentor, especially with women of color. I encouraged them to embrace their voices, to challenge stereotypes, and to redefine professionalism.

One evening, as the sun dipped below the city skyline, I sat alone in my department. My performance review awaited me—the same old feedback, I assumed. But this time, it was different.

"Willie Mae," my supervisor began, "your impact is undeniable. You've shattered glass ceilings and inspired us all. Keep being unapologetically you."

Tears welled in my eyes. I had to tighten my cheeks to prevent myself from crying. I'd fought not just for myself, but for every black woman who'd been told to soften her edges. I turned bias into fuel, and I taught them that professionalism wasn't about conformity—it was about authenticity, resilience, and unwavering belief in justice.

And so, in the hallowed halls of the firm, my legacy grew—a beacon for those who dared to combat stereotypes and rise, unapologetically, against the odds.

Black women have faced various stereotypes and biases throughout history. Here are some notable ones:

- **The "Angry Black Woman" Stereotype:**

This stereotype portrays black women as more hostile, aggressive, overbearing, illogical, ill-tempered, and bitter. Studies show that people in organizations often associate black women with belligerent, contentious, and angry personalities, a perception not as readily assigned to other men and women. When black women outwardly express anger at work, their leadership and potential may be questioned[1].

- **Welfare Queen Stereotype:**

Depicts black women as dependent on government assistance, perpetuating negative assumptions about their work ethic and financial responsibility.

- **Sapphire Caricature:**

Popular from the 1800s through the mid-1900s, it portrayed black women as sassy, emasculating, and domineering, violating social norms[1].

- **Threat and Danger Associations:**

Research shows that Black women and girls are more associated with threat and danger than White women and girls[2].

Label #2: "The Ice Queen"

In the heart of downtown Pittsburgh, where office towers reached for the sky and fluorescent lights hummed in sterile corridors, I worked in a great law firm. I was an Account Manager with a mind that dissected numbers like a surgeon's scalpel. But my brilliance came at a cost.

I had learned early in my career that vulnerability was a liability. I masked my insecurities with a stern expression, my lips always pressed into a thin line. My colleagues whispered behind my back, calling me the "Ice Queen." They didn't know the real Willie Mae—the stutterer, the one who was bi-polar, stayed up late, wrestling with self-doubt and the fear of being exposed.

One day, during a team meeting, my boss addressed the elephant in the room. "Willie Mae," he said, his tone gentle, "you're incredibly talented, but people find it hard to approach you. We need teamwork, not just brilliance."

My heart sunk. I had rehearsed that moment—the moment when my armor cracked—but I hadn't expected it so soon. I nodded; my throat tight.

He continued, "I want you to attend a workshop on effective communication. It's not about changing who you are; it's about enhancing your impact."

I reluctantly attended the workshop. The room was filled with people— men and women—eager to improve their interpersonal skills. The facilitator, a warm-hearted woman named Dr. Patel, began with a simple exercise: sharing personal stories.

As I listened to others, I realized I wasn't alone. The stern project manager had lost her father recently, and her aloofness was a shield against grief. The brilliant coder struggled with imposter syndrome, fearing that one day, someone would discover he was a fraud. And the quiet receptionist had once been ridiculed for her accent, leading her to withdraw.

Dr. Patel's words resonated: "We all carry our broken teacups. But vulnerability isn't weakness—it's strength. When we share our stories, we mend not only ourselves but also the fabric of our teams."

I took a deep breath and shared my fears—the fear of being labeled "mean," the fear of not fitting in. Tears surprised me, but they flowed freely. The room embraced my vulnerability, and I felt lighter.

Over the weeks that followed, I practiced empathy. I listened more than I spoke, and I noticed the subtle cues—the coworker who needed encouragement, the intern who felt lost. I learned that kindness wasn't a sign of weakness; it was a bridge connecting hearts.

Slowly, I thawed. I smiled more, and my colleagues noticed. They saw me as a mentor, not just an Account Manager. When I made mistakes, I owned them, and my team rallied around her.

One day, my boss called me into his office. "Willie Mae," he said, "you've transformed. You're still brilliant, but now you're also approachable. Keep mending those teacups."

And so, I continued my journey—a woman who embraced her imperfections, who wore her vulnerability like a badge of honor. I mentored young women, encouraging them to speak up, to be unapologetically themselves.

In the end, it wasn't just about me, Willie Mae—it was about every woman who dared to break the mold, to shatter the icy facade, and to mend their teacups together.

Supporting Black Women and Removing the Labels

Supporting black women is not just a matter of equity; it's a catalyst for enriching workplaces and driving innovation. To this end, there are several actionable steps that can be taken. Advocating for equal opportunities is paramount, which includes ensuring pay equity and promoting the advancement of black women into leadership roles. Additionally, establishing mentorship programs can provide guidance and empowerment, while sponsorship can open doors to new opportunities by advocating for black women in meetings and recommending them for key roles.

Amplifying the voices of black women is also crucial. This can be done by acknowledging their expertise and contributions, as well as inviting them to speak at panels, conferences, and discussions. Addressing microaggressions is another critical step, which involves educating colleagues about their impact and creating safe spaces where black women feel heard and respected.

Implementing flexible policies can further support black women by offering work arrangements that accommodate work-life balance and providing comprehensive parental leave. Lastly, cultural competency training that includes bias awareness can help employees recognize and address their biases, fostering a more inclusive and supportive work environment for black women. Together, these steps can lead to a more diverse, equitable, and innovative future.

Throughout history, black women have confronted harmful stereotypes and biases. These misconceptions can impact their self-esteem, mental health, and opportunities for success. However, by challenging these biases and *promoting understanding, we can create a more equitable and inclusive world.*

References

1. https://hbr.org/2022/01/the-angry-black-woman-stereotype-at-work

2. https://www.apa.org/news/press/releases/2020/07/black-women-social-justice

DR. ELIZABETH A. CARTER

Willie Mae Starr-White is Your Empathy Messenger, *"Turning Uncertainty into Silver Linings of Hope."* She is a motivational speaker with a passion for inspiring positive change.

For the past 17 years, she has been an active member of Toastmasters International, a community that has nurtured her love for communication and leadership. Through countless speech contests, she has honed her craft, learning that words can transform lives.

Starr-White's journey extends beyond the stage. As the co-author of four best-selling books, she has explored the depths of human resilience, personal growth, and the art of overcoming obstacles. These books are not just ink on paper; they represent shared wisdom, collective experiences, and the unwavering belief that we can all rise above our challenges.

Willie Mae balances her speaking and writing with a presence in the corporate world, spending the past 13 years as the Facilities/Office Services Manager at a prestigious law firm. In this role, she has witnessed the ebb and flow of professional life—the late nights, the early mornings, and the quiet moments when decisions shape destinies.

Are you looking for your silver lining?

Reach out to Willie Mae Starr-White at:

yourempathymessenger@gmail.com

linkedin.com/in/willie-mae-starr-whitea8b51a43

DR. ELIZABETH A. CARTER

CHAPTER 7

When Makeup Doesn't Cover the Story Behind the Pain

BY YVONNE WILBORN

" There is no greater agony than bearing an untold story."

~Maya Angelou

Dear Sisters,

On average, twenty people per minute are physically abused by an intimate partner in the United States. This equates to more than ten million women and men in a year[1].

This statistic is validated every day when I turn my television on and hear that someone was beaten or worse their life was taken because of domestic violence. This affects me personally because it brings back childhood memories of when I witnessed my stepfather abusing my mother. I vowed to never become a victim but unfortunately, I became a victim as well.

Now being a former domestic violence victim and survivor, my look on life seen through my eyes is to be cherished by the grace of God "I made it," out alive. Not everybody does. I have come to realize that there is no help in an untold story, so I must highlight the challenges of what I have learned as a survivor of domestic violence.

From my experiences, I will share stories, signs, consequences, and strategies to help you move forward in life. I will take you on several journeys about domestic violence. I want to create awareness of this hidden problem, it does not discriminate against gender, age, occupation, trade, or industry. I have found that many are not aware of the signs.

While I will be painting descriptive pictures of situations, the actual names are omitted to protect their privacy.

The Stories

Story #1

I met a longtime friend in the mall for lunch. We had not seen each other in years, and she was pregnant with her third child. She had her daughter with her, and wow, she was a gorgeous little girl. With the most beautiful piercing green eyes and mesmerizing skin color, she almost looked animated. She was breathtaking. I envisioned her future as a model, even a movie star. Her beauty came from her mother of course. She also had a son at home and not with her and his sister at the time. We spent at least two hours talking and having lunch together. Time flew by very quickly, and we knew we had to get back to our families. We hugged each other and we went our separate ways. Once I return home, my ritual is to turn on the television and have it play in the background after leaving the living room. I hear there is a hostage standoff unfolding. I ran back into the room and sat down to watch; SWAT and hostage negotiators were going back and forth talking to the individual trying to get the hostages released. After about 15 minutes I realized that it was my friend, checking my watch to see that it was not even an hour ago that we left the mall. Unfortunately, she, her son, her unborn child, and that gorgeous little girl that I had just met for the first time were killed. The crazy thing was that my friend did not show any sign that she was struggling with any domestic abuse.

Story #2

About thirty-three years ago, some friends and I were in a club. A gentleman walked in and noticed his girlfriend dancing with someone.

We were not sure how he was going to react, but he quickly left, so we assumed nothing and continued enjoying ourselves. To our surprise, he soon returned with a gun and shot the guy dancing with his girlfriend in the hand. Everyone panicked not knowing what he would do next and started running for the door. The shooter then shot his girlfriend, let her drop on the sidewalk, then turned around and shot her friend in the chest. I held the young lady's hand while she was lying on the sidewalk, a bullet lying right beside her. She had the most beautiful hair, and it was spread all over the sidewalk. I did not want his face to be the last face that she saw. At the same time, the other young lady's uncle was tending to her inside the club. Both women were transported to the hospital where they both passed. The young man who was shot in the hand was fine after he got help. The families of the victims formed a posse and refused to let the shooter leave the neighborhood until he was found (inside someone's garage) and arrested. This shows how life can be changed in an instant. A few minutes prior, I had taken what would now be the last picture of the two young ladies together. As there was chaos all around us, I recall the last song playing. The song was "Lately" by Stevie Wonder and every time I hear this song it stops me in my tracks, and sometimes I shed tears. This is something that I will never forget. Witnessing this event is one of the reasons why I am advocating against domestic violence.

Story #3

In 2012, I had the opportunity to interview a young lady who confided in me about her abusive relationship. She informed me that he was physically, verbally, and emotionally abusive and needed my help. Different steps were taken for her safety and to make sure that she got the help she needed. I also informed her that once she decides to move forward, she must be sure that this is something that she wants to do. There could very well be repercussions behind not going through with the protection once he is served with the protection from abuse order (PFA). Protection from Abuse is a civil law designed to protect individuals who have experienced or are threatened with physical or sexual violence. The PFA includes instructions that the abuser stay a certain distance from the victim. Depending on how severe the situation is an emergency PFA is granted by the judge[2] . It usually lasts one to three years, but a judge can extend the time limit. During the time we worked to complete the filing steps, I continued to inform her that if she did not want to file this PFA, do not file it. The reason for the reminders about filing the PFA is that sometimes feelings still exist for the abuser. After leaving the office, she felt good about filing the PFA (did I mention that we both were escorted to the office by the police so that the PFA could be filed quickly and in case her abuser showed up at her workplace?). Some time had passed since we completed the filing, and I happened to see her. She informed me that she was still with her boyfriend. She claimed everything was fine and she was doing well. I did not question her decision because I wanted her to stand on her decision and hers alone.

The Signs and Consequences

My Corporate Sisters, domestic violence is not always recognized, nor always visible. There are numerous signs that you are in an abusive relationship. Control, isolation, and fear are just to name a few. Domestic abuse is not limited to physical abuse. There is also verbal, emotional, and sexual abuse.

Physical Signs

Whether you are a survivor or a victim of an abusive relationship, we tend to shield and cover our pain. Here are examples of signs that could be a signal that abuse exists:

- Black eyes

- Covering scars with makeup

- Rings around one's neck.

- Wearing turtlenecks in the summertime

Emotional Signs

- Silence is something that victims know all too well. You are afraid to speak to anyone while with your abuser. Visiting family and friends is out of the question with some abusers. That is because your abuser will not be able to control you when you are out of their sight. Another way that your abuser controls you, have you ever gone to a family function and did not enjoy yourself? That is because you do not know how to enjoy yourself. You have been under so much control that it is impossible. Until you decide to give it up and move on with your life, you will continue to suffer in silence.

Consequences

- Suffering in silence can cause illnesses and depression.

- When a partner keeps their struggles to themselves, they begin to feel disconnected, and lack of communication can cause problems. Then you begin to feel isolated from the outside world. You begin to have stress and anxiety issues.

- For those with children, they are suffering just as much as their parents. When my son was three years old, he was my motivation to remove myself from my domestic situation. Sometimes you lose sight of yourself, he became my focus point and that is when I said, "Enough is enough." There were so many reasons why I did not want my son to see such behavior. The main reason is that he should never think that women are supposed to be treated in this manner. The other is that seeing this type of behavior in the household may leave your children with nervousness and stress. Also jeopardized is their confidence level and other things that aid the normal growth process of a child.

The Strategies

Corporate Sisters, I hope that by sharing what has happened in my life, I will be able to open your eyes to domestic violence. I hope I provided you with the ability to grow, build confidence, and find the strength to have a positive and fulfilling life. Things that I have learned during my abuse are:

- Never think that you are stuck in that awful position for the rest of your life. It feels like an eternity when you are being mistreated.

- Love is not supposed to hurt, and some think that being hit is a sign of love. Oh, but it is quite the opposite because love is hugging, kissing, holding hands, etc.

- Always make sure that you take care of yourself, and do not let anyone mistreat you.

- Never be afraid to speak up for yourself,

- If you need help, reach out to your family and friends. Suffering in silence when being abused is one of the most horrific things you can do in a relationship.

- Never take any of your past relationship dilemmas into a new one. Your information does not and should not be shared.

- Find a way to communicate your feelings and seek support. Counseling or therapy would be a good place to start addressing these issues.

- Makeup does not cover up the pain. If you, or someone that you know is in a domestic violence situation, please contact The Women's Center and Shelter of Greater Pittsburgh at 412-687-8005 (or the comparable service in your city), or the National Domestic Violence Hotline 24/7 at 800-799-7233

References

1. Statistics- NCADV- http://ncadv.org/Statistics

2. What is a protection from abuse order (PFA)- https://www.womenslaw.org

Dedicated to the memory of my mother

Viola Wilborn

And my stepmother

LaVerne Edmonds

Yvonne Wilborn is a Domestic Violence Confidante dedicated to supporting individuals affected by domestic violence. During her internship with the Pittsburgh Bureau of Police, she had the opportunity to tour the domestic violence unit. It was at that moment that she realized her calling to be an advocate against domestic violence.

After earning her bachelor's degree from the University of Pittsburgh in 2017, she created a platform to assist men and women in transforming from paralyzed victims to powerful victors.

Wilborn has received a certificate from the Pittsburgh Police Citizens Academy and a certificate of completion from the Pittsburgh Bureau of Police. Following her internship, she was honored with a proclamation to the city from The Honorable William Peduto.

In addition to her advocacy work, she organized a fundraiser for the Women's Center and Shelter by selling T Shirts to show her support for the shelter.

Wilborn has worked in customer service at the University of Pittsburgh for over 20 years. Her personal experience as a former domestic violence victim has given her the strength and voice to inspire and motivate survivors and those struggling with domestic violence.

If you want to talk further about domestic violence, please contact Yvonne at yvonnewilborn682@gmail.com or search for 'Bonnie's DV Strugglers'

ACKNOWLEDGMENTS

Thank you to the co-authors for their transparency in sharing their letters and lessons so that we can cultivate the leaders of generations to come. Thank you to those who have directly or indirectly shaped our lives so that we are able to stand here today powerfully blessed. Thank you to all contributors behind the scenes that allowed this vision to come together, and a special thanks to all the supporters who have purchased this book. May your life be shifted, and your success be fruitful.

WANT TO BE A CO-AUTHOR AND SHARE YOUR LETTER IN THE NEXT VOLUME?

If so, sign up for my VIP Community at

www.eac-aappeal.com

OR

Send an email to info@DrElizabethCarter.com, with the subject line – 'Letters to my Corporate Sisters- Next Volume' to get the details for the next project.

Make an impact on the world! Be the resource you did not have in your journey! Tell YOUR story to empower other women!

REFLECTION

Dear Sisters, now that you have read your letters, take time to write down your thoughts. Consider these questions.

- What situations are still lingering in your soul that make you question whether you are good enough to be a corporate sister?

- What stories/ideas/recommendations/quotes/scriptures will assist in shifting that current thinking?

- What new goals will you set?

- What will you do differently starting tomorrow?

Please write clear strategies for yourself and find an accountability coach.

MY NOTES

_____

_____

_____

_____

_____

_____

_____

_____

_____

_____

_____

_____

_____

LETTERS TO MY CORPORATE SISTERS

Made in the USA
Middletown, DE
21 September 2024

60856033R00066